Canadian Citizenship Test Study Guide FILL-IN Questions + Seven Practice Exams

Angelo Tropea

ISBN-13: 978-1719250757
ISBN-10: 1719250758

"We have created a society where individual rights and freedoms, compassion and diversity are core to our citizenship. But underlying that idea of Canada is the promise that we all have a chance to build a better life for ourselves and our children."

- Justin Trudeau

Contents

Canadian Citizenship Test

If you are between the ages of 18 and 54 and wish to become a Canadian citizen, you are required to take the citizenship test.

In addition to being able to successfully communicate with CIC staff (Citizenship and Immigration Canada), you must also pass the citizenship written multiple-choice test. The test includes questions about Canadian history geography and the rights and responsibilities of Canadian citizenship.

All the questions in this book are derived from the study guide "Discover Canada: The Rights and Responsibilities of Citizenship" which is excellent and is provided free by Citizenship and Immigration Canada as the primary official source for study.

The purpose of this book is designed to help you remember the facts in that study guide. We suggest that you use this book together with the study guide so that you will learn enough to not only easily pass the citizenship test, but also become a more knowledgeable citizen of Canada.

Full information on Canadian citizenship and immigration, and the free study guide may be obtained from the CIC official site:

Citizenship and Immigration Canada

Citoyenneté et Immigration Canada

www.cic.gc.ca

The following choices contain Fill-in questions and answers and additional information which will help you remember what you need to know.

How to Study with This Book

This book has many questions in a Fill-in question format. All the questions have been derived from the Official book, "Discover Canada: The Rights and Responsibilities of Citizenship", " The questions are designed to help you remember the information you need to know to pass the test.

Study all the Fill-in questions before you do the practice exams. Keep track of questions that you answer incorrectly. Focus on them more until you get them right. Do not write the answers or otherwise mark-up the book. This way you can retake the tests without being influenced by your previous answers.

This book and the "Discover Canada: The Rights and Responsibilities of Citizenship" are a good combination. These two study resources, if used properly, will eliminate the negative "test surprise" factor and increase your chances of doing well.

Try to establish and maintain an efficient practice schedule, preferably every day for a set amount of time. There is a theory of learning which states that people remember most when they study and practice for short periods instead of one long period. Therefore, seven study and practice periods during the week are more effective than one period during the weekend.

As you take these quizzes and tests, make note of any questions which you answer incorrectly. Did you answer wrong because you read the question incorrectly or because you need to focus on that question more?

Try to spend more time on your weakest areas. Do not concentrate on areas that you are most comfortable with and that you already know.

In summary, please try to remember that your chances of success depend greatly on the time and effort that you put into preparing for the exam.

Put it in your mind that
YOU WILL SUCCEED!

FILL-IN QUESTION

Introduction We swear (or affirm) true allegiance to __________.
The person who personifies Canada is _____________ .
Immigrants and settlers have been coming to Canada for _____ years.
Canada is a federal state, a parliamentary democracy and ______________.

ANSWER

We swear (or affirm) true allegiance to Her Majesty Queen Elizabeth the Second, Queen of Canada.
The person who personifies Canada is Her Majesty Queen Elizabeth the Second, Queen of Canada.
Immigrants and settlers have been coming to Canada for 400 years.
Canada is a federal state, a parliamentary democracy and a constitutional monarchy.

FILL-IN QUESTION

To become a Canadian citizen, a person between the ages of 18 and 54 must have adequate knowledge of one of these two languages: ______________.
Taking the Citizenship Test To become a Canadian citizen, a person must learn about the history of _______.
For an applicant not to be required to write the citizenship test, the applicant must be at least ___ years old.
A Notice to Appear to Take the Oath of Citizenship is given to a citizenship applicant (when?) ____________.

ANSWER
To become a Canadian citizen, a person between the ages of 18 and 54 must have adequate knowledge of one of these t wo languages: English and French. Also, the person must also learn about the geography and democratic institutions of Canada, voting procedures, Canada's history, symbols, and responsibilities and rights of Canadian citizenship.
To become a Canadian citizen, a person must learn about the history of Canada.
For an applicant not to be required to write the citizenship test, the applicant must be at least 55 years old.
A Notice to Appear to Take the Oath of Citizenship is given to a citizenship applicant after the applicant passes the test.

FILL-IN QUESTION

At the Oath of Citizenship Ceremony, the applicant takes ______________.
If an applicant does not pass the Citizenship Test, the applicant ________________.
At the ceremony, an applicant for citizenship (3 things) ______________.
Citizenship Responsibilities and Rights Three sources of Canadian law are: ________________.

ANSWER
At the Oath of Citizenship Ceremony, the applicant takes the Oath of Citizenship.
If an applicant does not pass the Citizenship Test, the applicant receives a notification indicating the next steps.
At the ceremony, an applicant for citizenship: 1. takes the Oath of Citizenship. 2. signs a form called the "oath form". 3. is given the Canadian Citizenship Certificate.
Three sources of Canadian law are 1. the civil code of France 2. English common law and laws passed by the provincial legislatures and parliament 3. Great Britain's unwritten constitution

FILL-IN QUESTION

The Magna Carta, signed in 1215, is also known as ______________.
The Magna Carta ensures ________________.
The following freedoms are included in the Magna Carta: "Freedom of conscience and religion; Freedom of thought, belief, opinion and expression, including freedom of speech and of the press; Freedom of peaceful assembly; and ______.
A legal procedure designed to challenge the unlawful detention of a person by the state is known as a ________.

ANSWER

The Magna Carta, signed in 1215, is also known as the Great Charter of Freedoms.
The Magna Carta ensures freedom of conscience and religion.
The following freedoms are included in the Magna Carta: "Freedom of conscience and religion; Freedom of thought, belief, opinion and expression, including freedom of speech and of the press; Freedom of peaceful assembly; and Freedom of association
A legal procedure designed to challenge the unlawful detention of a person by the state is known as habeas corpus proceeding.

FILL-IN QUESTION

In 1982 the Canadian Constitution was amended to include the ____________.
The words "Whereas Canada is founded upon principles that recognize the supremacy of God and the rule of law-" are the first words in the ________.
The Canadian Charter of Rights and Freedoms was entrenched in the Constitution of Canada in the year ____.)
The ______________________ summarizes fundamental freedoms, including Official Language Rights and Minority Language Educational Rights.

ANSWER

In 1982 the Canadian Constitution was amended to include the Canadian Charter of Rights and Freedoms.
The words "Whereas Canada is founded upon principles that recognize the supremacy of God and the rule of law-" are the first words in the Canadian Charter of Rights and Freedoms.
The Canadian Charter of Rights and Freedoms was entrenched in the Constitution of Canada in the year 1982.)
The Canadian Charter of Rights and Freedoms summarizes fundamental freedoms, including Official Language Rights and Minority Language Educational Rights. (Also, Mobility Rights, Aboriginal Peoples' Rights, and Multiculturalism.)

FILL-IN QUESTION

Men and women in Canada have ________ rights under the law.
Citizenship responsibilities include: obeying the law, serving on a jury, and (4 more) _____________.
In Canada military service is not _________.
<u>Canadian Peoples: Who We Are</u> Canadian Aboriginal peoples migrated from Asia (when?) ____________.

ANSWER

Men and women in Canada have <u>the same</u> (equal) rights under the law. Persons who are guilty of crimes such as "honour killings" and other similar criminal acts are punished by Canadian law.
Citizenship responsibilities include: obeying the law, serving on a jury, and: 1. <u>voting in elections</u> 2. <u>taking responsibility for oneself and one's family</u> 3. <u>helping others in the community</u> 4. <u>protecting and enjoying our heritage and environment.</u>
In Canada military service is not <u>compulsory</u>. Serving in the Canadian Forces or helping in the community is voluntary.
Canadian Aboriginal peoples migrated from Asia <u>many thousands of years ago.</u> The Canadian Constitution contains aboriginal and treaty rights. (King George III made the Royal Proclamation of 1763 which stated the basis for negotiating treaties between the aboriginals and newcomers.)

FILL-IN QUESTION

The three groups referred to in with the term Aboriginal Peoples are _____________.

_____________ said that immigrant groups "should retain their individuality and each make its contribution to the national character" and that immigrant groups could learn "from the other, and ... while they cherish their own special loyalties and traditions, they cherish not less that new loyalty and tradition which springs from their union."

Some Nations people live in about 600 communities on _______.

The name ______ means "the people." They speak the Inuktitut language and live in the arctic region.

ANSWER

The three groups referred to in with the term Aboriginal Peoples are Indian (First Nations), Inuit and Métis. (From about 1800 – 1980, children of aboriginal peoples were forced to be educated in residential schools. This led to some abuses and the schools were not successful.)

John Buchan, 1st Baron Tweedsmuir and Governor General of Canada from 1935 – 1940 said that immigrant groups, “should retain their individuality and each make its contribution to the national character” and that immigrant groups could learn “from the other, and ... while they cherish their own special loyalties and traditions, they cherish not less that new loyalty and tradition which springs from their union.”

Some Nations people live in about 600 communities on reserve land.
Others live off-reserve, usually in urban areas.

The name Inuit means “the people.” They speak the Inuktitut language and live in the arctic region.
The arctic is a harsh environment. To live there, the Inuit have accumulated great knowledge about the wildlife and land of the arctic.

FILL-IN QUESTION

The people that are comprised of Aboriginal and European ancestry are called ______.
The Métis make up about ___ % of the Aboriginal peoples.
The two official languages of Canada are __________.
In 1604 French colonists started settling in the Maritime provinces. The descendants of these settlers are called _________.

ANSWER

The people that are comprised of Aboriginal and European ancestry are called Métis. The Métis have both English speaking and French speaking backgrounds, but also speak their own Michif dialect.
The Métis make up about 30% of the Aboriginal peoples. First Nations (65%), Métis (30%), Inuit (4%) Aboriginal peoples are those whose ancestors migrated to Canada from Asia thousands of years in the past.
The two official languages of Canada are English and French. (18 million English speaking "Anglophones" and 7 million French speaking "Francophones.") Most French speaking people reside in the province of Quebec. One province (New Brunswick) is the only province that is officially bilingual.
In 1604 French colonists started settling in the Maritime provinces. The descendants of these settlers are called Acadians. Two thirds of Acadians were deported from their living area between 1755 and 1763 (This is referred to as "The Great Upheaval" of the Britain/French war.)

FILL-IN QUESTION

People of Quebec are called Quebecers. Most speak French, but about one million Anglo-Quebecers speak _________.
Recent immigrants to Canada (since 1970) come from ________. (continent)
In two of the largest cities of Canada, English is the most widely spoken language at home, followed by the non-official languages of ______.
<u>History of Canada</u> The first Europeans that explored Canada called the native people Indians because they believed that they were in the ________.

ANSWER

People of Quebec are called Quebecers. Most speak French, but about one million Anglo-Quebecers speak English. Anglo-Quebecers are descendants of Irish, Welsh, Scottish and English settlers. They are usually called English Canadians.
Recent immigrants to Canada (since 1970) come from Asia. Because of Canada's immigration, Canada is also spoken of as being the "land of immigrants." The most numerous people living in Canada are: English, French, Scottish, Irish, German, Italian, Chinese, Aboriginal, Ukrainian, Dutch, South Asian, and Scandinavian.
In two of the largest cities of Canada, English is the most widely spoken language at home, followed by the non-official languages of Chinese.
The first Europeans that explored Canada called the native people Indians because they believed that they were in the East Indies. Some Indians were hunters, farmers, nomadic and some were hunter-gatherers.

FILL-IN QUESTION

After Aboriginals came into contact with Europeans, many died of diseases to which they lacked __________.
The name of the people that colonized Greenland (1,000 years ago) and also set foot on Newfoundland and Labrador is _________.
The name Canada comes from an Iroquoian (Indian) word kanata, which means _______.
In 1604 European settlements were established by French explorers Pierre de Monts and ___________.

ANSWER

After Aboriginals came into contact with Europeans, many died of diseases to which they lacked immunity. In spite of this, in the first 200 years of Canada's history, there developed military and economic bonds between the Aboriginals and the settlers.
The name of the people that colonized Greenland (1,000 years ago) and also set foot on Newfoundland and Labrador is Vikings. Also, in 1497 John Cabot (Italian immigrant to England) drew a map of Canada's east coast. Also, Jacques Cartier (French) between 1534 and 1542 claimed the land for the King of France, King Francis I.
The name Canada comes from an Iroquoian (Indian) word kanata, which means village. The name "Canada" first appeared on maps.
In 1604 European settlements were established by French explorers Pierre de Monts and Samuel de Champlain. The settlements were established on St. Croix Island and Port-Royal. (St. Croix Island is in Maine (US) and at Port-Royal in Acadia (Canada).

FILL-IN QUESTION

Samuel de Champlain made an alliance with the _________ Indians.
The company that King Charles II (1670) granted exclusive trading rights in the Hudson Bay area was __________.
The British defeated the French in ______ in the Battle of the Plains of Abraham at Quebec City. This ended the French Empire in America.
The people living in the "Province of Quebec" under the English speaking British Empire are known as _______________ .

ANSWER

Samuel de Champlain made an alliance with the Huron, Montagnais and Algonquin. The Iroquois and the French battled for almost a century. They made peace in the year 1701. (The Iroquois were enemies with the Huron, Montagnais and Algonquin.) The Aboriginal peoples and the French established a fur-trade economy. Under the leadership of leaders such as Count Frontenac, Jean Talon and Bishop Laval, the French Empire spread from the Atlantic coast (Hudson Bay) to the Gulf of Mexico.
The company that King Charles II (1670) granted exclusive trading rights in the Hudson Bay area was Hudson's Bay Company. Furs were often collected by traders who often travelled by canoe. They formed agreements with the First Nations. These traders are referred to as "coureurs des bois" and "voyageurs".
The British defeated the French in 1759 in the Battle of the Plains of Abraham at Quebec City. This ended the French Empire in America. Brigadier James Wolfe led the British soldiers and the Marquis de Montcalm led the French soldiers. They were both killed in the battle.
The people living in the "Province of Quebec" under the English speaking British Empire are known as habitants or Canadiens. In 1774, the British Parliament passed the "Quebec Act of 1774." This act permitted the French speaking Catholic people to hold public office. This act also established French civil law and English criminal law.

FILL-IN QUESTION

Around 1776 people loyal to the Crown fled the thirteen American colonies and settled in Nova Scotia and Quebec. These people were called _________.
The Act in 1791 which divided the Province of Quebec into Upper Canada (present day Ontario) and Lower Canada (present day Quebec) is known as ___________________.
Slavery was abolished first in the province of Upper Canada in 1793. Its first Lieutenant Governor was Lieutenant Colonel John Graves Simcoe. He founded the City of York whose present-day name is _________.
Mary Ann (Shadd) Carey, the first woman publisher in Canada, in 1853 founded and edited the Provincial Freeman, which encouraged ___________________________.

ANSWER

Around 1776 people loyal to the Crown fled the thirteen American colonies and settled in Nova Scotia and Quebec. These people were called Loyalists.
Some of these black Loyalists (freed slaves) settled in Nova Scotia, but in 1792 moved to Africa and established Freetown in Sierra Leone (West Africa).

The Act in 1791 which divided the Province of Quebec into Upper Canada (present day Ontario) and Lower Canada (present day Quebec) is known as The Constitutional Act of 1791.
Upper Canada was mainly English speaking and Lower Canada was mainly French speaking.
"British North America" generally referred to the two Canadas (Upper and Lower) and the Atlantic colonies.

Slavery was abolished first in the province of Upper Canada in 1793. Its first Lieutenant Governor was Lieutenant Colonel John Graves Simcoe. He founded the City of York whose present-day name is Toronto.
In 1807 the buying and selling of slaves was abolished by the British Parliament, who also in 1833 abolished throughout the empire the buying and selling of slaves.

Mary Ann (Shadd) Carey, the first woman publisher in Canada, in 1853 founded and edited the Provincial Freeman, which encouraged anti-slavery and black immigration to Canada.
She also encouraged the support of British rule and drinking less alcohol.

FILL-IN QUESTION

In the 1800's Canadian financial institutions began to emerge. In 1832 the __________ Stock exchange opened.
The _______ invaded Canada in the year 1813.
The rebellion of _________ occurred mainly because some people thought that democracy was not coming fast enough to Canada.
The person who suggested that Lower Canada and Upper Canada be merged and given "responsible government" was ____________.

ANSWER

In the 1800's Canadian financial institutions began to emerge. In 1832 the Montreal Stock exchange opened. Before the 1800's the economy of Canada relied mostly on its natural resources (fish, timber, furs, etc.) and on farming.
The USA invaded Canada in the year 1813 (during the War of 1812). In 1813 the Americans burned Government House and Parliament buildings in present day Toronto. In 1814 the British burned the White House and other government buildings in Washington D.C. The border between the U.S. and Canada is one of the results of the War of 1812.
The rebellion of 1837-38 occurred mainly because some people thought that democracy was not coming fast enough to Canada. Also, some Canadians were in favour of joining the United States.
The person who suggested that Lower Canada and Upper Canada be merged and given "responsible government" was Lord Durham. "Responsible government" that Lord Durham recommended meant that the ministers of the Crown in order to govern needed the support of the majority of the elected representatives of the Canadian people. (He mistakenly suggested that all Canadiens needed to be assimilated into the culture of the English Protestants.)

FILL-IN QUESTION

The Province of Canada was the result of the 1840 unification of ________________________.
The Dominion of Canada was established by the __________ in 1867.
On July 1, 1867 the Fathers of Confederation established Canada. July 1 was celebrated as "Dominion Day" until 1982. However today "Dominion Day" is called ____________.
Nanavut joined Canada in the year _____

ANSWER

The Province of Canada was the result of the 1840 unification of Upper and Lower Canada. "Responsible government" in the Province of Canada was advanced by reformers such as Robert Baldwin, Sir Louis-Hippolyte La Fontaine and Joseph Howe. In 1848-49 responsible government was introduced in Canada by Lord Elgin, governor of United Canada.
The Dominion of Canada was established by the Fathers of Confederation in 1867. Two levels of government (federal and provincial) were introduced.
On July 1, 1867 the Fathers of Confederation established Canada. July 1 was celebrated as "Dominion Day" until 1982. However today "Dominion Day" is called Canada Day. The term "Dominion of Canada" was suggested by Sir Leonard Tilley, one of the Fathers of Confederation, in the year 1864.
Nanavut joined Canada in the year 1999. (1867) Ontario, Quebec, Nova Scotia, New Brunswick (1870) Manitoba, Northwest Territories (N.W.T.) (1871) British Columbia (1873) Prince Edward Island (1880) Transfer of Arctic Islands to N.W.T (1898) Yukon Territory (1905) Saskatchewan, Alberta (1949) Newfoundland and Labrador (1999) Nanavut

FILL-IN QUESTION

Canada's first Prime Minister (1867) was ___________.
A patriotic Canadien, this person was from Quebec and a key architect of Confederation: _____________.
Prime Minister Macdonald in 1873 established the __________________.
The first French-Canadian prime minister since confederation, Sir Wilfrid Laurier, is on the _____ bill.

ANSWER

Canada's first Prime Minister (1867) was Sir John Alexander Macdonald. Sir John Alexander Macdonald's portrait is on the $10 bill. On January 11 we celebrate Sir John A. Macdonald Day.
A patriotic Canadien, this person was from Quebec and a key architect of Confederation: Sir George-Etienne Cartier Sir George-Etienne Cartier also was instrumental in the negotiations for the following territories to enter into Canada: Manitoba, Northwest Territories, and British Columbia.
Prime Minister Macdonald in 1873 established the NWMP (North West Mounted Police). The NWMP (now RCMP: Royal Canadian Mounted Police) are Canada's national police force. The NWMP were established after the first Métis uprising. Two great Métis leaders were Louis Riel (father of Manitoba) and Gabriel Dumont.
The first French-Canadian prime minister since confederation, Sir Wilfrid Laurier, is on the $5 bill. Sir Wilfrid Laurier encouraged people to immigrate to the West. Immigration was also helped by the railway from Sea to Sea, completed in 1885. It was built mostly by European and Chinese labour.

FILL-IN QUESTION

The person known as "Canada's greatest soldier" is ________________.
The founder of the woman's suffrage movement in Canada was ____________.
Remembrance Day is observed on ___________.
The British Commonwealth of Nations is a free association of ________.

ANSWER

The person known as "Canada's greatest soldier" is Sir Arthur Currie. Sir Arthur Currie fought in WWI. Canadian troops also volunteered to fight in the South African War (1899-1902).
The founder of the woman's suffrage movement in Canada was Dr. Emily Stowe. Nurses were granted the right to vote in 1917 and most Canadian female citizens over 21 in 1918.
Remembrance Day is observed on November 11. On Remembrance Day we remember the sacrifice of 110,000 Canadians who have given their lives in wars by wearing the red poppy and observing a moment of silence. The poem "In Flanders Fields" was composed by Lt. Col. John McCrae. It was composed in 1915 and is recited on Remembrance Day.
The British Commonwealth of Nations is a free association of states. The Commonwealth includes Australia, India, some African countries and some Caribbean countries.

FILL-IN QUESTION

In the _______ battle, one in ten of the Allied soldiers was Canadian.
<u>Modern Canada</u> The Act which guarantees health insurance coverage is _______________.
The Act which guarantees French language rights and services in all of Canada is ____________________________.
The "Group of Seven" (founded in 1920) developed a ___________________.

ANSWER

In the D-Day battle, one in ten of the Allied soldiers was Canadian. In the second World War (1939-1945), more than one million Canadians and Newfoundlanders served in the military, including air and naval forces.
The Act which guarantees health insurance coverage is The Canada Health Act. Unemployment insurance was introduced in 1940 by the federal government. Education is provided by the provinces and territories.
The Act which guarantees French language rights and services in all of Canada is The Official Languages Act (1969). The Quebec sovereignty movement was defeated in two referendums (1980 and 1995).
The "Group of Seven" (founded in 1920) developed a style of painting.

FILL-IN QUESTION

The sport of basketball was invented by _________ in 1891.

The Canadian who invented the worldwide system of standard time zones was ______________.

The British North America Act of 1867 (now known as the Constitution Act, 1867) defined ____________________ ________________.

Canadian Government

Canada's type of government is a _________________.

ANSWER

The sport of basketball was invented by James Naismith in 1891. Sports in Canada are popular in all provinces. Canadian scientists have contributed greatly to the world.
The Canadian who invented the worldwide system of standard time zones was Sir Sandford Fleming. (Reginald Fassenden contributed to the invention of the radio. Alexander Graham Bell thought of the telephone while at his summer house in Canada. Dr. John A. Hopps invented the pacemaker).
The British North America Act of 1867 (now known as the Constitution Act, 1867) defined the responsibilities of the provincial and federal governments of Canada. Each province has a Legislative Assembly which it elects.
Canada's type of government is a parliamentary democracy. If the Cabinet ministers receive a "no-confidence" vote, they must resign.

FILL-IN QUESTION

The three parts of Parliament are: ____________________.
In the federal government, the ___________ selects Cabinet members and is responsible for government policy and operations.
When a bill is considered read for the first time and is printed, it is at step 1, called the __________.
Members debate and vote on a bill in the ___________.

ANSWER

The three parts of Parliament are: The Sovereign, the Senate, and House of Commons. The provinces have legislatures that are comprised of the elected Assembly and the Governor of the province.
In the federal government, the Prime Minister selects Cabinet members and is responsible for government policy and operations. The House of Commons is elected by the people every four years. Senators are appointed by the Prime Minister. Laws are passed by both chambers and royal consent (granted by the Governor General).
When a bill is considered read for the first time and is printed, it is at step 1, called the First Reading. There are 7 steps in how a bill becomes law: 1) First Reading, 2) Second Reading, 3) Committee Stage, 4) Report Stage, 5) Third Reading, 6) Senate, 7) Royal Assent.
Members debate and vote on a bill in the Report Stage. There are 7 steps in how a bill becomes law: 1) First Reading, 2) Second Reading, 3) Committee Stage, 4) Report Stage, 5) Third Reading, 6) Senate, 7) Royal Assent

FILL-IN QUESTION

The minimum age at which Canadians can vote is _____.
In Canada the head of state is the Sovereign. The head of government is the _____________.
The three branches of government are the Executive, Legislative and __________.
<u>Federal Elections</u> Members of the House of Parliament are also called ______ _________.

ANSWER

The minimum age at which Canadians can vote is 18. Canada is a Constitutional Monarchy. Canada's Head of State is the Sovereign The Commonwealth has 52-member states.
In Canada the head of state is the Sovereign. The head of government is the Prime Minister. The Governor General represents the Sovereign. Each of the 10 provinces has a Lieutenant Governor (appointed by the Governor General on the advice of the Prime Minister).
The three branches of government are the Executive, Legislative and Judicial. The Premier (of each province) is similar to the Prime Minister.
Members of the House of Parliament are also called MPs or Members of Parliament. Federal elections are held every 4 years (in October) following the most recent general election. The prime Minister can ask the Governor General to call an election sooner.

FILL-IN QUESTION

The MP (Member of Parliament) is chosen by the voters in an ____________________.
Elections Canada, a neutral agency of parliament produces a list called the ________________________.
The leader of the party with the most seats in the House of Commons forms the government (after being invited to do so by the Governor General). If that part holds at least half the seats in the House of Commons, the government is called the ___________ government.
The Cabinet is made up of the Prime Minister and the ______________.

ANSWER

The MP (Member of Parliament) is chosen by the voters in: an electoral district. Canada has 308 electoral districts (also called constituencies or ridings). MPs sit in the House of Commons. The minimum age to run in a federal election is 18.
Elections Canada, a neutral agency of parliament produces a list called the National Register of Electors. To vote in a federal election, a person must: 1. be a Canadian citizen 2. be at least 18 (on voting day) 3. be on the National Register of Electors
The leader of the party with the most seats in the House of Commons forms the government (after being invited to do so by the Governor General). If that party holds at least half the seats in the House of Commons, the government is called the majority government. (If it holds less than half the seats, it is called the minority government.) After a vote of "no confidence" the Prime Minister usually asks the Governor General to call for an election
The Cabinet is made up of the Prime Minister and the Cabinet ministers. The Cabinet makes decisions regarding how the country is run. These decisions may be questioned by the Official Opposition (Opposing party with the most members) and by parties not in power (known as opposition parties).

FILL-IN QUESTION

On a voting ballot, you mark an ___ to indicate the name of the candidate of your choice.

Canadian Justice System

Laws passed by local or municipal governments are called ________.

Presumption of innocence (everyone is innocent until proven guilty) is the foundation of our _________ system.

The highest court in Canada is the ________________.

ANSWER

On a voting ballot, you mark an X to indicate the name of the candidate of your choice.
Laws passed by local or municipal governments are called by-laws. Municipal or local governments have responsibilities in the following areas: policing, firefighting, emergency services, recycling programs, transportation, community affairs and community health and utilities.
Presumption of innocence (everyone is innocent until proven guilty) is the foundation of our judicial system. Courts settle disputes. Police enforce laws. Due process means that all the legal rights of a person must be respected by the government.
The highest court in Canada is the Supreme Court of Canada. (Provinces have a number of lesser courts.)

FILL-IN QUESTION

The ________________ police enforce federal laws and serve as the provincial police in all territories and provinces, except Quebec and Ontario.

Symbols of Canada

The Crown is a symbol of government, including the courts, the legislatures, the police services, the armed forces.

National Flag day is __________.

The most popular spectator sport in Canada is __________.

ANSWER

The Royal Canadian Mounted police enforce federal laws and serve as the provincial police in all territories and provinces, except Quebec and Ontario.
The Crown is a symbol of government, including the courts, the legislatures, the police services, the armed forces.
National Flag day is February 15. The Canadian flag was first raised on February 15, 1965. It has a red-white-red pattern. The Maple leaf is also a Canadian symbol. The coat of arms and the motto "A Mari Usque Ad Mare" which means "from Sea to Sea" are used on currency, public buildings and government documents.
The most popular spectator sport in Canada is ice hockey. The second most popular sport is Canadian football. The sport with the most registered players is soccer.

FILL-IN QUESTION

The animal that is on the five-cent coin is the ________.
The National anthem of Canada is "__________."
The highest honour that a Canadian can receive is ___________.
Sir John A. Macdonald Day is celebrated on __________.

ANSWER

The animal that is on the five-cent coin is the beaver.
The National anthem of Canada is "O Canada." (The "Royal Anthem" is sung whenever the Queen is to be honored.) Citizens who are worthy of recognition are awarded the "Order of Canada."
The highest honour that a Canadian can receive is The Victoria Cross (V.C.).
Sir John A. Macdonald Day is celebrated on January 11. Vimy Day – April 9 Victoria Day – Monday preceding May 25 (Sovereign birthday) Fete Nationale (Quebec) June 24 (Feast of St. John the Baptist)

FILL-IN QUESTION

Remembrance Day is celebrated on ____________.
Economy of Canada Today more than 75% of Canadians are employed in ________ industries.
The biggest trading partner of Canada is __________.
The second largest country in the world is ________.

ANSWER

Remembrance Day is celebrated November 11. Also remember: Sir Wilfrid Laurier Day – November 20 Christmas – December 25 Boxing Day – December 26
Today more than 75% of Canadians are employed in Service industries.
The biggest trading partner of Canada is the U.S.A. The U.S.A. and Canadian border is the world's longest undefended border.
The second largest country in the world is Canada. Canada is bordered by the Atlantic Ocean, Pacific Ocean and the U.S.A.

FILL-IN QUESTION

Regions of Canada Canada has ___ distinct regions.
The national capital of Canada is ________.
Canada has ___ provinces.
The population of Canada is about ___ million.

ANSWER

Canada has 5 distinct regions. 1. The Atlantic Provinces 2. The Prairie Provinces 3. The Northern Territories 4. Ontario and Quebec 5. The West Coast
The national capital of Canada is Ottawa. (In 1857 Queen Victoria chose Ottawa as the capital.)
Canada has 10 provinces. Canada has 10 provinces and 3 territories. (Memorize the capitals of your province or territory and the capital of Canada.)
The population of Canada is about 34 million. Most Canadians live in cities.

FILL-IN QUESTION

The capital of Nova Scotia is ________.
The capital of Ontario is ________.
____________________________ is the location of the oldest colony. It is the province with the most easterly point is North America, and also known for its fisheries.
The only officially bilingual province is ______________.

ANSWER

The capital of Nova Scotia is Halifax. Also, Mewfoundland and Labrador – St. John's New Brunswick – Fredericton Prince Edward Island - Charlottetown
The capital of Ontario is Toronto. Quebec – Quebec City Manitoba – Winnipeg Saskatchewan – Regina Alberta – Edmonton British Columbia – Victoria Nanavut – Igaluit Northwest Territories – Yellowknife Yukon Territory - Whitehorse
Newfoundland and Labrador are the location of the oldest colony. It is the province with the most easterly point is North America, and also known for its fisheries. The smallest province is Prince Edward Island. The Atlantic province with the most population is Nova Scotia.
The only officially bilingual province is New Brunswick. Most people in Canada (more than half) live in Ontario and Quebec. In Quebec three-quarters of the people speak French as their first language.

FILL-IN QUESTION

Nanavut and Yukon (Northwest Territories) contain a population of ________ but comprise 1/3 of Canada's land.
The three provinces known as the Prairie Provinces are Manitoba, Alberta and ____________.
The Prairie Province that is most populous is Alberta.
The Port of Vancouver is found in the Province of ____________.

ANSWER

Nanavut and Yukon (Northwest Territories) contain a population of only 100,000 but comprise 1/3 of Canada's land. During the 1890's gold rush, thousands of minors came to the Yukon in search of treasure. .
The three provinces known as the Prairie Provinces are Manitoba, Alberta and Saskatchewan. Saskatchewan is known as the "breadbasket of the world" and the "wheat province."
The Prairie Province that is most populous is Alberta. The Province was named after Princess Louise Caroline Alberta, the fourth daughter of Queen Victoria.
The Port of Vancouver is found in the Province of British Columbia. Chinese and Punjabi are spoken often in the cities, next to English.

FILL-IN QUESTION

Other Study Questions

Our rights and freedoms are contained in two key documents

1. The Magana Carta
2. ________________.

The following are four rights that Canadians enjoy:

1. Mobility rights
2. Aboriginal People's rights
3. Official language rights and Minority language rights
4. ________________.

Four (4) freedoms that Canadians enjoy are:

1. Freedom of expression, thought, opinion, belief, freedom of press, and of speech
2. Freedom of association
3. Freedom of conscience and religion
4. ___________________________

In Canada men and women have ______ rights under the law. Cultural practices of other countries that promote inequality are NOT allowed in Canada. Abuse of men or women is punished by Canadian criminal law.

ANSWER

Our rights and freedoms are contained in two key documents

1. The Magana Carta
2. The Constitution of Canada.

The following are four rights that Canadians enjoy:

1. Mobility rights
2. Aboriginal People's rights
3. Official language rights and Minority language rights
4. Multiculturalism.

Four (4) freedoms that Canadians enjoy are:

1. Freedom of expression, thought, opinion, belief, freedom of press, and of speech
2. Freedom of association
3. Freedom of conscience and religion
4. Freedom of peaceful assembly

In Canada men and women have equal rights under the law. Cultural practices of other countries that promote inequality are NOT allowed in Canada. Abuse of men or women is punished by Canadian criminal law.

FILL-IN QUESTION

Some examples of taking responsibility for yourself and your family include: 1. _______ 2. obeying the law 3. serving on a jury 4. taking responsibility for one's family and oneself. 5. volunteering in the community, or volunteering to serve or defend Canada.
___________ peoples migrated to Canada from Asia. They were in Canada long before the first explorers (that is, Vikings and then English speaking and French-speaking Christian settlers).
The _______ are people of mixed European and Indian ancestry.
_____________ Government means that the ministers of the crown in order to govern need the consent of the majority of the elected Canadian representatives.

ANSWER

Some examples of taking responsibility for yourself and your family include: 1. Voting 2. obeying the law 3. serving on a jury 4. taking responsibility for one's family and oneself. 5. volunteering in the community, or volunteering to serve or defend Canada.
Aboriginal peoples migrated to Canada from Asia. They were in Canada long before the first explorers (that is, Vikings and then English speaking and French-speaking Christian settlers).
The Métis are people of mixed European and Indian ancestry.
Responsible Government means that the ministers of the crown in order to govern need the consent of the majority of the elected Canadian representatives.

FILL-IN QUESTION

Sir __________________________ was the first leader of the Canadas responsible government. He struggled for democracy and French language rights.
The ________________ Railway symbolized Canadian unity. Confederation means the birth of Canada on July 1, 1867.
__________ was discovered by Sir Frederick Banting and Charles Best. Their discovery helped save 16 million miles.
In a ______________ Monarchy the Head of State is a hereditary King or Queen who reigns in accordance with law (the Constitution).

ANSWER

Sir Louis-Hippolyte La Fontaine was the first leader of the Canadas responsible government. He struggled for democracy and French language rights.
The Canadian Pacific Railway symbolized Canadian unity. Confederation means the birth of Canada on July 1, 1867.
Insulin was discovered by Sir Frederick Banting and Charles Best. Their discovery helped save 16 million miles.
In a Constitutional Monarchy the Head of State is a hereditary King or Queen who reigns in accordance with law (the Constitution).

FILL-IN QUESTION

There are three branches of government:

1. the Executive
2. Legislative
3. _________

Canada is a **Constitutional Monarchy**.
The Head of State is a hereditary Sovereign (King or Queen). The King or Queen reigns in accordance with the Constitution of Canada.
The Head of Government is the ____________. The Prime Minister is the person who is responsible for running the government.

The highest honour that Canadians can receive is the ______________.

On election day you vote for the candidates of your choice. You go to the polling station with your identification and voter information card.
On the ballot (the voting sheet) you mark an "___" next to the candidates of your choice

ANSWER

There are three branches of government:

1. the Executive
2. Legislative
3. Judicial

Canada is a **Constitutional Monarchy**.
The Head of State is a hereditary Sovereign (King or Queen). The King or Queen reigns in accordance with the Constitution of Canada.
The Head of Government is the Prime Minister. The Prime Minister is the person who is responsible for running the government.

The highest honour that Canadians can receive is the Victoria Cross (V.C.).

On election day you vote for the candidates of your choice. You go to the polling station with your identification and voter information card.
On the ballot (the voting sheet) you mark an "**X**" next to the candidates of your choice

FILL-IN QUESTION

In Canadian federal elections a person may vote if the person:

1. is a Canadian citizen, AND
2. is at least ____ years old on voting day, and
3. is on the voter's list.

In Canada you are not obliged to tell anyone how you voted.

After an election the political party with the greatest number of seats in the ____________________ is invited by the Governor General to form a government.

The three levels of government are:

1. Federal
2. Provincial and Territorial
3. _______________

The courts in Canada guarantee that everyone receives due process under the law.
In Canada you are allowed to question the police about their service or conduct.

The following four provinces are referred to as the "Atlantic Provinces"?

1. Newfoundland and Labrador
2. Prince Edward Island
3. Nova Scotia
4. _______________

ANSWER

In Canadian federal elections a person may vote if the person: 1. is a Canadian citizen, AND 2. is at least 18 years old on voting day, and 3. is on the voter's list. In Canada you are not obliged to tell anyone how you voted.
After an election the political party with the greatest number of seats in the House of Commons is invited by the Governor General to form a government.
The three levels of government are: 1. Federal 2. Provincial and Territorial 3. Municipal (local) The courts in Canada guarantee that everyone receives due process under the law. In Canada you are allowed to question the police about their service or conduct.
The following four provinces are referred to as the "Atlantic Provinces"? 1. Newfoundland and Labrador 2. Prince Edward Island 3. Nova Scotia 4. New Brunswick

Provinces and Capitals

Atlantic Provinces Region

Province / Territory	Capital City
Newfoundland and Labrador	St. John's
Prince Edward Island	Charlottetown
New Brunswick	Fredericton
Nova Scotia	Halifax

Central Canada

Quebec	Québec City
Ontario	Toronto

Prairie Provinces

Manitoba	Winnipeg
Saskatchewan	Regina
Alberta	Edmonton

West Coast

British Columbia	Victoria

North

Northwest Territories	Yellowknife
Yukon	Whitehorse
Nanavut	Iqaluit

Government

The 4 main levels of government in Canada are:

1. Municipal government,
2. Territorial government,
3. Provincial government, and
4. Federal government

1. MUNICIPAL GOVERNMENT

Name of municipality of residence	
Mayor or Reeve of municipality of residence	

2. TERRITORIAL GOVERNMENT

Commissioner (Federal government representative)	
Premier	
Territorial Representative	

3. PROVINCIAL GOVERNMENT

Lieutenant Governor (Representative of the Queen	
Premier (Head of Government):	
Provincial Party in Power	
Provincial Opposition Leader	
Provincial Representative	

4. FEDERAL GOVERNMENT

Governor General (the representative of the Queen of Canada	
Prime Minister of Canada	
Political Party in Power	
Leader of the Opposition	
Name of Loyal Opposition Party	
Other Opposition Parties and Leaders Are	
My MP (Member of Parliament) is	
My federal electoral district is	

Important dates

DAY	DATE
New Year's Day	January 1
Sir John A. Macdonald Day	January 11
Good Friday	Friday immediately preceding Easter Sunday
Easter Monday	Monday immediately following Easter Sunday
Vimy Day	April 9
Victoria Day	Monday preceding May 25 (Sovereign's birthday)
Fête Nationale (Quebec)	June 24 (Feast of St. John the Baptist)
Canada Day	July 1
Labour Day	First Monday in September
Thanksgiving Day	Second Monday in October
Remembrance Day	November 11
Sir Wilfrid Laurier Day	November 20
Christmas	December 25
Boxing Day	December 26

PRACTICE TEST 1

1. We swear (or affirm) allegiance to:
A. the constitution
B. the flag
C. Canada
D. Her Majesty Queen Elizabeth the Second, Queen of Canada

2 At the Oath of Citizenship Ceremony, the applicant:
A. must write the test.
B. must answer 20 questions.
C. receives a Canadian passport.
D. takes the Oath of Citizenship.

3. A legal procedure designed to challenge the unlawful detention of a person by the state is known as:
A. subpoena
B. detention
C. habeas corpus
D. release

4. Men and women in Canada:
A. have different rights under the law.
B. are equal under the law.
C. are never equal under the law.
D. are sometimes equal under the law.

5. Who said that immigrant groups, "should retain their individuality and each make its contribution to the national character" and that immigrant groups could learn "from the other, and ... while they cherish their own special loyalties and traditions, they cherish not less that new loyalty and tradition which springs from their union."
A. John Buchan, 1st Baron Tweedsmuir and Governor General of Canada from 1935 – 1940.
B. King Henry III
C. Lord Durham
D. Sir George Cartier

6. Two Canadian official languages are:
A. English and Spanish
B. English and French
C. French and Spanish
D. Spanish and English

7. The first Europeans that explored Canada called the native people _______ because they believed that they were in the East Indies.
A. Europeans
B. Asians
C. Indians
D. South Americans

8. Samuel de Champlain made an alliance with:
A. the Iroquois
B. Huron, Montagnais and Algonquin
C. the Apaches
D. the Comanche, Apaches and Blackfeet

9. Which Act in 1791 divided the Province of Quebec into Upper Canada (present day Ontario) and Lower Canada (present day Quebec)?
A. The Constitutional Act of 1791.
B. The Freedom Act of 1791.
C. The Compromise Act of 1791.
D. The Canada Agreement Act of 1791.

10. The rebellion of 1837-38 occurred mainly because people thought that:
A. Canada should be divided.
B. Canada should be a dictatorship.
C. democracy was not coming fast enough to Canada.
D. Canada should join with Mexico.

11. Which of the following groups became part of Canada first?
A. Ontario, Quebec, Nova Scotia, New Brunswick
B. Manitoba, Northwest Territories (N.W.T.)
C. British Columbia
D. Prince Edward Island

12. The person known as "Canada's greatest soldier" is:
A. Sir Arthur Currie
B. Emily Stowe
C. John Macdonald
D. Pierre Amiens

13. The Act which guarantees health insurance coverage is:
A. The Suffrage Act
B. The Employment Act
C. The Canada Health Act
D. The Act of Independence

14. The British North America Act of 1867 (now known as the Constitution Act, 1867):
A. extended health care to all Canadians.
B. made peace with the U.S.A.
C. defined the responsibilities of the provincial and federal governments of Canada.
D. provided for the Canadian railway.

15. In this legislative step, Members debate and vote on a bill:
A. First Reading
B. Second Reading
C. Third Reading
D. Report Stage

16. Elections Canada, a neutral agency of parliament produces a list called:
A. National Register of Electors
B. National List
C. Election List
D. National Emergency List

17. On a voting ballot, what do you mark to indicate the name of the candidate of your choice?

A. AOK
B. Y
C. X
D. G

18. Which of the following is a symbol of government, including the courts, the legislatures, the police services, the armed forces?

A. the parliament building
B. the Crown
C. the star
D. the flag of Maine

19. Which of the following holiday dates is NOT correct?

A. New Year's Day – January 1
B. Sir John A. Macdonald Day – February 11
C. Good Friday – Friday immediately preceding Easter Sunday
D. Easter Monday – Monday following Easter Sunday

20. Canada has ___ distinct regions.

A. 3
B. 4
C. 5
D. 7

END: (Answers on pg. 105)

PRACTICE TEST 2

1. Who personifies Canada?
A. every citizen
B. The Prime Minister
C. Minister of Public Works
D. our Sovereign

2. If an applicant does not pass the Citizenship Test, the applicant:
A. loses his filing fee.
B. cannot take the test ever again.
C. must sign the oath form.
D. receives a notification indicating the next steps.

3. In 1982 the Canadian Constitution was amended to include the Canadian _____.
A. Charter of Rights and Freedoms.
B. Magna Carta.
C. Liberties Manifesto.
D. Law of Citizenship.

4. Which of the following is not a citizenship responsibility?
A. obeying the law
B. serving on a jury
C. voting in elections
D. participating in sports

5. Some Nations people live in about 600 communities:
A. on reserve land.
B. in Toronto
C. in Quebec
D. in urban centres.

6. In 1604 French colonists started settling in the Maritime provinces. The descendants of these settlers are called ______.
A. aboriginals
B. Acadians
C. nationals
D. Anglophones

7. After Aboriginals came into contact with Europeans, many died of diseases to which they lacked __________.
A. contact
B. immunity
C. agreement
D. time

8. The company that King Charles II (1670) granted exclusive trading rights in the Hudson Bay area was called:
A. Hudson's Bay Company
B. Fur Traders, Inc.
C. Canada Fur Trading
D. Furs of Canada Company

9. Slavery was abolished first in the province of Upper Canada in 1793. Its first Lieutenant Governor was Lieutenant Colonel John Graves Simcoe. He founded the City of York whose present-day name is _________.
A. Quebec City
B. Toronto
C. Harrisburg
D. Montreal

10. The person who suggested that Lower Canada and Upper Canada be merged and given "responsible government" was:
A. Lord Durham
B. John Cabot
C. Major General Robert Ross
D. John Graves

11. Which of the following groups became part of Canada first?
A. Ontario, Quebec, Nova Scotia, New Brunswick
B. Manitoba, Northwest Territories
C. British Columbia
D. Prince Edward Island

12. The founder of the woman's suffrage movement in Canada was:
A. Emile Bronte
B. Dr. Emily Stowe
C. Nancy Baker
D. Harriet Beecher

13. Which Act guarantees French language rights and services in all of Canada?
A. The Suffrage Act
B. The Canada Act.
C. The Official Languages Act
C. The Commonwealth Act

14. Canada's type of government is:
A. an oligarchy
B. a federalist dictatorship
C. a parliamentary democracy
D. socialist

15. The minimum age at which Canadians can vote is.
A. 14
B. 18
C. 21
D. 22

16. The leader of the party with the most seats in the House of Commons forms the government (after being invited to do so by the Governor General). If that part holds at least half the seats in the House of Commons, the government is called:
A. the minority government
B. the majority government
C. the government elect
D. compromise government

17. Laws passed by local or municipal governments are called:
A. by-laws
B. major laws
C. federal laws
D. in-laws

18. National Flag of Canada Day is:
A. February 15
B. March 15
C. April 15
D. May 15

19. Which of the following holiday date is NOT correct?
A. Canada Day – July 1
B. Labour Day – First Monday of September
C. Thanksgiving Day – Second Monday of October
D. Remembrance Day – November 15

20. The national capital of Canada is:
A. Montreal
B. Toronto
C. Ottawa
D. Milburn

END: (Answers on pg. 105)

PRACTICE TEST 3

1. Immigrants and settlers have been coming to Canada for:
A. 200 years
B. 300 years
C. 400 years
D. 500 years

2. Which of the following is false?
At the ceremony, an applicant for citizenship:
A. takes the Oath of Citizenship.
B. signs a form called the "oath form".
C. is given the Canadian Citizenship Certificate.
D. must pay a citizenship fee.

3. The words "Whereas Canada is founded upon principles that recognize the supremacy of God and the rule of law-" are the first words in:
A. the Constitution of Canada.
B. the Magna Carta.
C. the Freedom Manifesto.
D. the Habeas Corpus Act.

4. In Canada:
A. military service is not compulsory.
B. you must serve in the military.
C. you must serve in the Coast Guard.
D. you must serve in the fire department.

5. The name of this group means "the people." They speak the Inuktitut language and live in the arctic region.
A. Métis
B. Inuit
C. Apache
D. Acadians

6. People of Quebec are called Quebecers. Most speak French, but about one million Anglo-Quebecers speak ____.
A. English
B. Spanish
C. Arabic
D. French

7. What is the name of the people that colonized Greenland (1,000 years ago) and also set foot on Newfoundland and Labrador?
A. English
B. French
C. Vikings
D. Asians

8. The British defeated the French in _____ in the Battle of the Plains of Abraham at Quebec City. This ended the French Empire in America.
A. 1600
B. 1759
C. 1812
D. 1845

9. Mary Ann (Shadd) Carey, the first woman publisher in Canada, in 1853 founded and edited the Provincial Freeman, which encouraged:
A. separation from British rule.
B. expansion of Canadian territories.
C. anti-slavery and black immigration to Canada.
D. annexation of western territories.

10. The Province of Canada was the result of the 1840 unification of:
A. Quebec and Montreal
B. Toronto and Vancouver
C. Upper and Lower Canada
D. Montreal and Toronto

11. Prime Minister Macdonald in 1873 established:
A. the NWMP (North West Mounted Police).
B. Fort Garry
C. Montreal
D. Hudson's Bay Company

12. The British Commonwealth of Nations is a free association of states. It evolved:
A. in the 1700's.
B. in 1886
C. after the First Word War.
D. in 2004.

13. The "Group of Seven" (founded in 1920) developed:
A. a style of painting
B. military maneuvers
C. educational resources
D. political parties

14. The three parts of Parliament are: The Sovereign, the Senate, and:
A. House of Commons
B. Constitutional Convention
C. Cabinet
D. local assembly

15. In Canada the head of state is the Sovereign. The head of government is:
A. the Senators
B. the Assembly
C. the Prime Minister
D. the Governors

16. The Cabinet is made up of the Prime Minister and the ______.
A. Assemblymen
B. Cabinet ministers
C. Senators
D. royal assembly

17. Presumption of innocence (everyone is innocent until proven guilty) is the foundation of:
A. our judicial system
B. our political system
C. our philosophical system
D. our executive branch

18. The most popular spectator sport in Canada is:
A. baseball
B. ice hockey
C. football
D. swimming

19. Today more than 75% of Canadians are employed in:
A. Manufacturing industries
B. Service industries
C. Fishing Industry
D. Entertainment industry

20. Canada has ____ provinces.
A. 8
B. 10
C. 11
D. 12

END: (Answers on pg. 105)

PRACTICE TEST 4

1 Which of the following choices is not correct? Canada is:
A. a federal state
B. a parliamentary democracy
C. a dictatorship
C. a constitutional monarchy

2. Which of the following is NOT a source of Canadian law?
A. the civil code of France
B. English common law and laws passed by the provincial legislatures and parliament
C. Great Britain's unwritten constitution
D. laws enacted by the North Atlantic Treaty Organization.

3. The Canadian Charter of Rights and Freedoms was entrenched in the Constitution of Canada in the year ____.
A. 1812
B. 1814
C. 1982
D. 2009

4. Canadian Aboriginal peoples migrated from Asia:
A. in the 1800's
B. In the twelfth century
C. many thousands of years ago
D. In the 1970's

5. The people that are comprised of Aboriginal and European ancestry are called:
A. Inuit
B. First nation
C. Indian
D. Métis

6. Recent immigrants to Canada (since 1970) come from _____.
A. Europe
B. Africa
C. Asia
D. South America

7. The name Canada comes from an Iroquoian (Indian) word "kanata," which means:
A. country
B. river
C. house
D. village

8. The people living in the "Province of Quebec" under the English speaking British Empire are known as:
A. English
B. habitants or Canadiens
C. citizens
D. inhabitants

9. In the 1800's Canadian financial institutions began to emerge. In 1832 the _____ Stock exchange opened.
A. Johnston
B. Winnipeg
C. Toronto
D. Montreal

10. The Dominion of Canada was established by the Fathers of Confederation in 1867. Which of the following are Fathers of Confederation?
A. Lord Durham, John Cabot, Major General Robert Ross
B. Sir Étienne-Paschal Taché, Sir George-Étienne Cartier, Sir John A. McDonald
C. Sir Louis-Hippolyte La Fontaine, John Cabot, Major General Robert Ross
D. Sir Isaac Brock, John Cabot, Étienne Durham

11. The first French-Canadian prime minister since confederation, Sir Wilfrid Laurier, is on which the following bills?
A. $1 bill
B. $5 bill
C. $10 bill
D. $20 bill

12. On Remembrance Day we wear a red poppy. Remembrance Day is observed on:
A. January 21
B. April 15
C. November 11
D. June 8

13. The sport of basketball was invented by:
A. Donovan Bailey in 1886.
B. Chantal Peticlerc
C. James Naismith in 1891
D. Wayne Gretsky

14. In the federal government, who selects Cabinet members and is responsible for government policy and operations?
A. the Senators
B. the Assembly
C. the Prime Minister
D. the Governors

15. The three branches of government are the Executive, Legislative and:
A. the people
B. the cabinet
C. Judicial
D. committees

16. The House of Commons presently has members of four major political parties: The Liberal Party, the New Democratic Party, the Bloc Quebecois, and:
A. the Conservative Party.
B. Populist Party.
C. Green Party.
D. Independent Party.

17. The highest court in Canada is:
A. Provincial Court
B. Supreme Court of Canada
C. Trial Court
D. City Court

18. The animal that is on the five-cent coin is the:
A. pigeon
B. eagle
C. bear
D. beaver

19. The biggest trading partner of Canada is:
A. Mexico
B. England
C. U.S.A.
D. Japan

20. The population of Canada in 2010 is approximately:
A. 20 million
B. 34 million
C. 60 million
D. 120 million

END: (Answers on pg. 105)

PRACTICE TEST 5

1. The only officially bilingual province is:
A. New Brunswick
B. Ontario
C. Quebec
D. Nova Scotia

2. The largest city in Canada is Toronto. It is located in the province of:
A. Quebec
B. Ontario
C. Manitoba
D. Newfoundland and Labrador

3. To become a Canadian citizen, a person between the ages of ______ must have adequate knowledge of French or English.
A. 21 and 62
B. 18 and 54
C. 16 and 55
D. 21 and 54

4. The Magna Carta, signed in 1215, is also known as :
A. the Constitution
B. the amendment
C. the Great Charter of Freedoms
D. the First Law

5. The Canadian Charter of Rights and Freedoms summarizes fundamental freedoms, including Official Language Rights and Minority Language Educational Rights. Under this charter:
A. all languages are official languages
B. French is the only official language
C. English is the only official language
D. Both French and English are official languages.

6. The three groups referred to in with the term Aboriginal Peoples are:
A. Comanche, Aztec and Huron.
B. Indian (First Nations), Inuit and Métis.
C. French, English, Dutch
D. Lakota, Comanche and Mayan.

7. Which of the following percentages relating to Aboriginal people are correct?
A. First Nations (65%), Métis (30%), Inuit (4%)
B. First Nations (33%), Métis (33%), Inuit (33)
C. First Nations (25%), Métis (25%), Inuit (50%)
D. First Nations (40%), Métis (40%), Inuit (20%)

8. In two of the largest Canadian cities, English is the most widely spoken language at home, followed by ______.
A. Italian
B. Greek
C. Lithuanian
D. Chinese

9. In 1604 European settlements were established by French explorers Pierre de Monts and:
A. Vasco de Gama
B. Samuel de Champlain
C. Christopher Columbus
D. Vikings

10. Around 1776 people loyal to the Crown fled the thirteen American colonies and settled in Nova Scotia and Quebec. They were called ______.
A. settlers
B. escapees
C. Loyalists
D. soldiers

11. The USA invaded Canada in the year _____.
A. 1776
B. 1789
C. 1812
D. 1860

12. On July 1, 1867 the Fathers of Confederation established Canada. July 1 was celebrated as "Dominion Day" until 1982. However today "Dominion Day" is called:
A. Unity Day
B. Canada Day
C. Constitution Day
D. Liberty Day

13. In this battle, one in ten of the Allied soldiers was Canadian.
A. Battle of Hastings
B. Battle of 1887
C. D-Day
D. 1976

14. The Canadian who invented the worldwide system of standard time zones was:
A. Alexander Graham Bell
B. Reginald Fassenden
C. Dr. John A. Hopps
D. Sir Sandford Fleming

15. When a bill is considered read for the first time and is printed, it is at step 1, which is called the:
A. First Reading
B. Second Reading
C. Third Reading
D. Report Stage

16. Members of the House of Parliament are also called:
A. MPs or Members of Parliament
B. Dukes
C. Earls
D. Commoners

17. Which of the following police enforce federal laws and serve as the provincial police in all of Canada, except Quebec and Ontario?
A. the city police
B. the Royal Canadian Mounted police
C. the town and village police
D. the military police

18. The National anthem of Canada is:
A. Our Country
B. O Canada
C. Forever Canada
D. Everywhere Canada

19. The second largest country in the world is:
A. China
B. U.S.A.
C. Canada
D. Brazil

20. Which of the following is NOT the correct capital for the province or territory listed?
A. Newfoundland and Labrador – St. John's
B. Nova Scotia – Halifax
C. New Brunswick – Fredericton
D. Prince Edward Island - Albany

END: (Answers on pg. 105)

PRACTICE TEST 6

1. Which of the following choices is NOT correct? To become a Canadian citizen, a person must learn about:
A. U.S. history
B. geography of Canada
C. Canada's history
D. responsibilities of Canadian citizenship

2. How old does an applicant have to be to not be required to write the citizenship test?
A. 18 C. 55
B. 21 D. 34

3. Which of the following rights are included in the Magna Carta?
1. Freedom of Association
2. Freedom of conscience and religion.
A. none of them
B. both freedoms are included in the Magna Carta.
C. Only A. Freedom of Association
D. Only B. Freedom of conscience and religion

4. Canada's first Prime Minister (1867) was:
A. Sir George-Étienne Cartier
B. Sir Sam Steele
C. Sir John Alexander Macdonald
D. Gabriel Dumont

5. A patriotic Canadien from Quebec and a key architect of Confederation was:
A. Sir George-Étienne Cartier
B. Sir Sam Steele
C. Sir John Alexander Macdonald
D. Gabriel Dumont

6. The MP (Member of Parliament) is chosen by the voters in:
A. a province
B. an electoral district
C. A town
D. a city

7. The highest honour that a Canadian can receive is:
A. The Victoria Cross (V.C.)
B. The Medal of Honour
C. The Canadian Medal
D. The Victory Cross

8. Which of the following is NOT the correct capital for the province or territory listed?
A. Quebec – Quebec City
B. Ontario – Toronto
C. Manitoba – Winnipeg
D. Saskatchewan – King

9. The two provinces known as the Prairie Provinces are:
A. Manitoba and Saskatchewan
B. Quebec and Ontario
C. Labrador and Newfoundland
D. New Brunswick and Nova Scotia

10. The highest mountain in Canada is:
A. Mount McKinley
B. Mount Logan
C. Mount Sinai
D. Mount Pacific

11. The Magna Carta specifically ensures:
A. freedom from jail and paying taxes.
B. unfair factory labor.
C. freedom from taxes only.
D. freedom of conscience and religion.

12. The oldest colony and the province with the most easterly point is North America, and also known for its fisheries is the province of:
A. Prince Edward Island
B. Newfoundland and Labrador
C. Nova Scotia
D. New Brunswick

13. The Port of Vancouver is found in the Province of:
A. Alberta
B. British Columbia
C. Toronto
D. Quebec

14. The Prairie Province that is most populous is:
A. British Columbia
B. Alberta
C. Quebec
D. Ontario
15. Who personifies Canada?
A. every citizen
B. The Prime Minister
C. Minister of Public Works
D. our Sovereign

16. Which of the following choices is not correct? Canada is:
A. a federal state
B. a parliamentary democracy
C. a dictatorship
D. a constitutional monarchy

17. The people that are comprised of Aboriginal and European ancestry are called:
A. Inuit
B. First nation
C. Indian
D. Métis

18. The two official languages of Canada are:
A. English and Spanish
B. English and French
C. French and Spanish
D. Spanish and English

19. What is the name of the people that colonized Greenland (1,000 years ago) and also set foot on Newfoundland and Labrador?
A. English
B. French
C. Vikings
D. Asians

20. The company that King Charles II (1670) granted exclusive trading rights in the Hudson Bay area was called:
A. Hudson's Bay Company
B. Fur Traders, Inc.
C. Canada Fur Trading
D. Furs of Canada Company

END: (Answers on pg. 106)

PRACTICE TEST 7

1. We swear (or affirm) allegiance to:
A. the constitution
B. the flag
C. Canada
D. Her Majesty Queen Elizabeth the Second, Queen of Canada

2 At the Oath of Citizenship Ceremony, the applicant:
A. must write the test.
B. must answer 20 questions.
C. receives a Canadian passport.
D. takes the Oath of Citizenship.

3. A legal procedure designed to challenge the unlawful detention of a person by the state is known as:
A. subpoena
B. detention
C. habeas corpus
D. release

4. Which of the following is not a citizenship responsibility?
A. obeying the law
B. serving on a jury
C. voting in elections
D. participating in sports

5. Some Nations people live in about 600 communities:
A. on reserve land.
B. in Toronto
C. in Quebec
D. in urban centres.

6. In 1604 French colonists started settling in the Maritime provinces. The descendants of these settlers are called ______.
A. aboriginals
B. Acadians
C. nationals
D. Anglophones

7. What is the name of the people that colonized Greenland (1,000 years ago) and also set foot on Newfoundland and Labrador?
A. English
B. French
C. Vikings
D. Asians

8. The British defeated the French in _____ in the Battle of the Plains of Abraham at Quebec City. This ended the French Empire in America.
A. 1600
B. 1759
C. 1812
D. 1845

9. Mary Ann (Shadd) Carey, the first woman publisher in Canada, in 1853 founded and edited the Provincial Freeman, which encouraged:
A. separation from British rule.
B. expansion of Canadian territories.
C. anti-slavery and black immigration to Canada.
D. annexation of western territories.

10. The Dominion of Canada was established by the Fathers of Confederation in 1867. Which of the following are Fathers of Confederation?
A. Lord Durham, John Cabot, Major General Robert Ross
B. Sir Étienne-Paschal Taché, Sir George-Étienne Cartier, Sir John A. McDonald
C. Sir Louis-Hippolyte La Fontaine, John Cabot, Major General Robert Ross
D. Sir Isaac Brock, John Cabot, Étienne Durham

11. The first French-Canadian prime minister since confederation, Sir Wilfrid Laurier, is on which the following bills?
A. $1 bill
B. $5 bill
C. $10 bill
D. $20 bill

12. On Remembrance Day we wear a red poppy. Remembrance Day is observed on:
A. January 21
B. April 15
C. November 11
D. June 8

13. In this battle, one in ten of the Allied soldiers was Canadian.
A. Battle of Hastings
B. Battle of 1887
C. D-Day
D. 1976

14. The Canadian who invented the worldwide system of standard time zones was:
A. Alexander Graham Bell
B. Reginald Fassenden
C. Dr. John A. Hopps
D. Sir Sandford Fleming

15. When a bill is considered read for the first time and is printed, it is at step 1, called the:
A. First Reading
B. Second Reading
C. Third Reading
D. Report Stage

16. Which of the following choices is not correct? Canada is:
A. a federal state
B. a parliamentary democracy
C. a dictatorship
C. a constitutional monarchy

17. The people that are comprised of Aboriginal and European ancestry are called:
A. Inuit
B. First nation
C. Indian
D. Métis

18. The two official languages of Canada are:
A. English and Spanish
B. English and French
C. French and Spanish
D. Spanish and English

19. Which of the following holiday dates is NOT correct?
A. New Year's Day – January 1
B. Sir John A. Macdonald Day – February 11
C. Good Friday – Friday immediately preceding Easter Sunday
D. Easter Monday – Monday immediately following Easter Sunday

20. Canada has ___ distinct regions.
A. 3
B. 4
C. 5
D. 7

END: (Answers on pg. 106)

Practice Test Answers

Test 1

1. D	5. A	9. A	13. C	17. C
2. D	6. B	10. C	14. C	18. B
3. C	7. C	11. A	15. D	19. B
4. B	8. B	12. A	16. A	20. C

Test 2

1. D	5. A	9. B	13. C	17. A
2. D	6. B	10. A	14. C	18. A
3. A	7. B	11. A	15. B	19. D
4. D	8. A	12. B	16. B	20. C

Test 3

1. C	5. B	9. C	13. A	17. A
2. D	6. A	10. C	14. A	18. B
3. A	7. C	11. A	15. C	19. B
4. A	8. B	12. C	16. B	20. B

Test 4

1. C	5. D	9. D	13. C	17. B
2. D	6. C	10. B	14. C	18. D
3. C	7. D	11. B	15. C	19. C
4. C	8. B	12. C	16. A	20. B

Test 5

1. A	5. D	9. B	13. C	17. B
2. B	6. B	10. C	14. D	18. B
3. B	7. A	11. C	15. A	19. C
4. C	8. D	12. B	16. A	20. D

Test 6

1. A	5. A	9. A	13. B	17. D
2. C	6. B	10. B	14. B	18. B
3. B	7. A	11. D	15. D	19. C
4. C	8. D	12. B	16. C	20. A

Test 7

1. D	5. A	9. C	13. C	17. D
2. D	6. B	10. B	14. D	18. B
3. C	7. C	11. B	15. A	19. B
4. D	8. B	12. C	16. C	20. C

Notes

30496378R00061

Made in the USA
Lexington, KY
10 February 2019